The Indo-Pacific Li[illegible]

SRI LAN[illegible]

Graham Houghton & Julia Wakefield

CONTENTS

Jaffna
Jaffna Lagoon
INDIA
Mannar
Trincomalee
Puttalam
River
Mahaweli
Batticaloa
Kandy
Pidurutalagala
COLOMBO
Badulla
Kalutara
kilometres
100

Geography

In the distant past Sri Lanka was part of the greater Indian sub-continent. It is now separated from India by the Palk Strait, a distance of about 32 kilometres. However, a string of small sandy islands and coral reefs known as Adam's Bridge almost joins it to the mainland. Because of the closeness of India, it has always influenced events in Sri Lanka and the original inhabitants of the islands must have travelled there from southern India.

Sri Lanka measures about 435 kilometres north to south, and about 230 kilometres east to west at its widest point. Its southernmost tip is about 6° north of the Equator and only the great Southern Ocean separates it from the land mass of Antarctica.

The highest land is found in the centre of the island with Mount Pidurutalagala being the highest point. There are broad coastal plains with long stretches of sand dunes behind. Often fresh water is found here.

The Sri Lankan coastline

Waterfalls

Earth movements millions of years ago have pushed up parts of the island into a series of three steps. This has caused some difficulty in communications across the island, but it has also created spectacular waterfalls and the potential for valuable hydro-electric power schemes.

Overlooking the port of Kandy

About one-eighth of the country is above 300 metres above sea level and it is from this hill country that the rivers flow in all directions across the island. The longest river is Mahaweli Ganga which begins its 333 kilometre journey to the Indian Ocean near Adam's peak which rises to 2,236 metres. The rivers are an important source of water for irrigation and can be used for transportation by shallow draft boats. One of the tallest waterfalls on Earth is to be found in Sri Lanka. It is called the Koslanda Bridal Veil and falls some 212 metres. Sri Lanka depends for a large part of its income on tourism and one of the greatest attractions are its coral reefs which are popular with divers from all over the world.

Climate

Monsoons

The climate of Sri Lanka is equatorial, that is it has no clearly defined seasons. The temperature is fairly constant throughout the year and it is only with the arrival of the monsoons that weather conditions change to any great extent. The south-west monsoon lasts from May until August while the north-east monsoon occurs between November and January.

The Wet Zone and the Dry Zone

There are two main regions known as the wet zone, and the dry zone. The wet zone is to be found in the south-west and has a fairly constant rainfall throughout the year. The dry zone also has good rainfall in most years, but during the summer can be affected by drought. During the monsoons as much as 3,000 mm of rain can be dumped on towns in the hill country and this can lead to serious flooding in the lowlands with the loss of important crops.

During the south-west monsoon there often occurs a hot dry wind known to Sri Lankans as the Kachchan. This starts in the early morning and by mid-afternoon can be blowing at gale force. But by

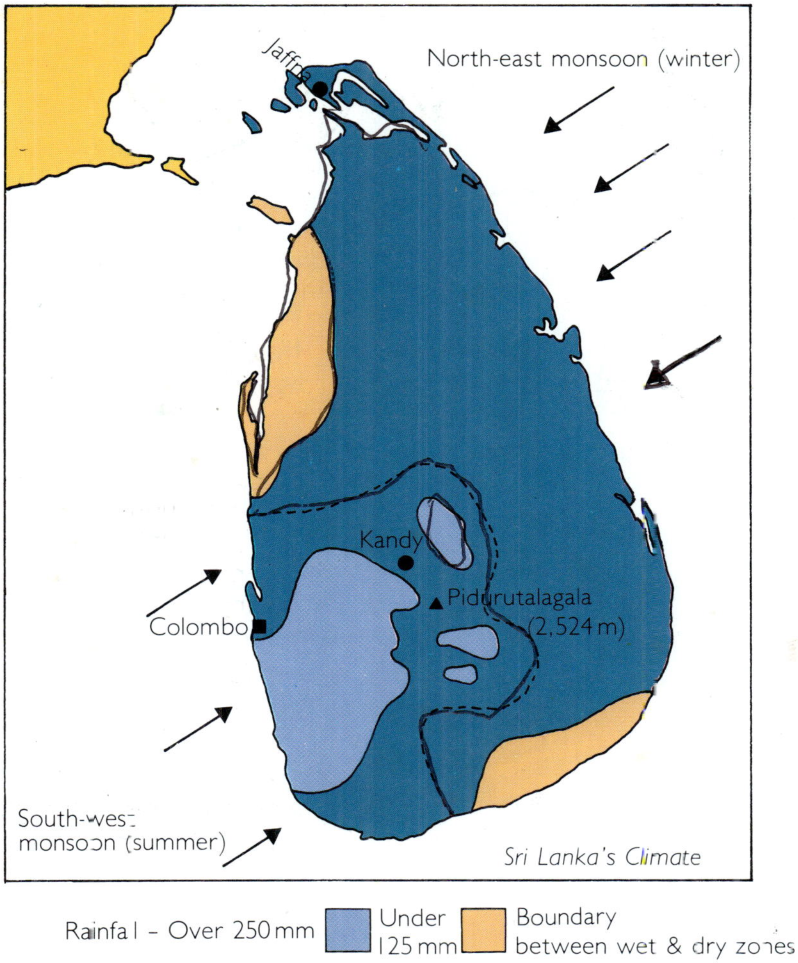

Sri Lanka's Climate

the time the sun drops it has usually subsided again. Similar winds occur in other parts of the world, for example in North Africa where such a wind is called the Sirocco.

Sri Lanka's climate is governed by a number of factors which include: its nearness to the Equator; being surrounded by sea which helps to modify any extremes of temperature; the monsoons; and its relief. In the hill country the temperature during the year is somewhat lower than on the coastal plains. Several hill stations have been built over the years with perhaps the most famous being Nuwara Eliya which stands in a wooded valley at about 1,900 metres above sea level. The mean daily temperature of Nuwara Eliya is about 16°C, but the temperature during the day is, of course, much higher. The British colonial rulers of Sri Lanka built a health resort and military hospital at Nuwara Eliya and even established an 'English village' complete with vegetable gardens and herds of pedigree English cattle.

Natural Resources

Sri Lanka has few mineral resources and no deposits of coal or oil.

Minerals

Graphite, a form of carbon, is the main mineral export and is mined in three locations: at Bogala, Kahatagaha, and Kalangaha. About 8,000 tonnes of graphite are produced each year. Export of llemite has also gained importance-current annual production is 100,000 MT.

Gemstones are also an important resource. They include rubies, sapphires, beryl, topaz and tourmaline. Most semi-precious stones are extracted from river deposits in the south-west of the country.

Limestone forms the basis for a local cement industry, while glass sands and rare earths are present in enough quantities for local needs also.

The oldest industry in Sri Lanka is that of salt extraction. The salt is produced from sea-water which is pumped into large lagoons and then evaporates in the heat of the sun to leave behind a thin crust of salt. Salt is used in Sri Lanka's chemical industry.

Energy

Although there are no reserves of fossil fuels, power is generated by hydro-electric schemes located mainly in the hill country.

Water

Water has long been recognised as a precious commodity in Sri Lanka and over hundreds of years thousands of dams of various sizes have been built. These dams are known as tanks, or *wewas*, and an intricate system of irrigation canals was built at the same time to bring water to the rice fields in villages. These ancient systems are still in use and are often integrated with fish farms.

Fisheries

Fishing is an important industry with the main catch coming from coastal waters. There are over 25,000 fishing boats based around the island. A large proportion of them are without motors and depend on sails or paddles for propulsion.

Nets are hauled in by the men of the village each morning

The Environment

Native Plants

All the non-cultivated areas in Sri Lanka are called 'jungle'. Before people arrived much of the island was covered in tropical forest, but with the clearing of forests for farming over the ages only about one fifth of the country still has this forest cover. Most of the forest is concentrated in the hill country, the low lying coastal plains having been cleared of the thick bush. Where forest has been destroyed a thick thorn scrub soon takes over. There are large areas of grassland known locally as *patanas*. These probably developed as a result of annual burning of the forest by the early farmers which prevented the original vegetation growing back.

Around the coast thick mangrove and bamboo forests grow, and most of the sandy beaches are fringed with coconut palms.

There are four main national parks where all wildlife is strictly protected. Three of these, the Uda Walawe, Yala, and Gal Oya Parks are in the south-east of the island, while the fourth, the Wilpattu Park lies to the north-west. There are also many especially protected areas where only scientific expeditions are allowed.

The Kelaniya River

Wildlife and National Parks

Because Sri Lanka has had Buddhism as its main religion for so long there has always been respect shown to wild animals.

In the twelfth century King Kirthi Nissanka Malla had a decree carved in stone: 'No animals should be killed within a radius of seven gaus from the city'. Bestowing on the people gold and cloth and whatever else they wished he commanded them not to catch

Elephants at work tourist carrying!

birds. Even today over one tenth of the island is under the direct protection of the government. Despite this, however, the Indian elephant, was once in danger of extinction because of over-hunting by ivory merchants. There is a separate group of elephants, known as marsh elephants, which live only along the banks of the Mahaweli River.

Four varieties of deer can be found in the National Parks along with large numbers of monkeys. One of the most spectacular monkey species has a purple face and is sometimes known as the bear monkey. At times large groups of them can be seen in an area known as Horton Plains. There are numerous squirrel species, including the flying squirrel, along with wild cats, hares and jackals. Wild boar and buffalo are common in many areas. Leopards are less frequently seen: but there were two cases of man-eating leopards earlier this century. The sloth bear feeds mainly on termites and honey, but has been known to attack man if surprised, or defending offspring.

Reptiles

Reptiles include the crocodile, the iguana, and the water monitor. There are also numerous poisonous snakes including the cobra, the krait, and vipers. The python is the largest snake to be found on the island. Around the coast turtles are regular visitors and a number of sanctuaries have been set up to protect them during their breeding season.

Giant bats are native to Sri Lanka

Bird Life

The variety of bird life on the island is great and reflects the widely differing environments found there. Numerous birds of prey hunt the smaller species. The mountain hawk eagle is confined to the hill country while the Brahiminy kite and the serpent eagle operate over a wider area. The sea eagle, of course, hunts around the coastline.

A large number of the water birds are seasonal migrants from other lands. These include flamingos, herons, godwits, sandpipers and various species of duck.

Peacocks are found in the low wooded country and a number of species can be found in both the country and the town: crows, pheasants, rollers, drongos, and whistlers.

People and History

The Veddas

The Veddas, whose name means 'hunters', were the original inhabitants of the island. It is not certain when the Veddas first arrived. Small communities of these people still live in parts which tend to be isolated. Even so, they are being absorbed into the rest of Sri Lankan life, and are disappearing as a distinct group.

The Sinhalese

The second arrivals were the Sinhalese who today form the bulk of the population. Ancient Buddhist texts suggest that they journeyed to Sri Lanka under the leadership of a Prince named Vijaya with the personal blessing of Buddha himself. This is said to have happened at the time of Buddha's death which occured in the sixth century B.C. The Sinhalese were an Aryan people and lived mainly by farming. Even today the main religion of the island is Buddhism.

This Buddhist frescoe in Sigiriya is 1500 years old

The Jaffna Tamils

Following the Sinhalese came the Jaffna Tamils who are a large minority living in the north. The Jaffna Tamils are a Dravidian people and probably began trade with the island from southern India as early as the third century B.C. A second and much larger group of Jaffna Tamils invaded Sri Lanka in about the thirteenth century bringing the Hindu religion with them. A third group of Tamils, known as Indian Tamils, were taken to the island in the nineteenth century to work on the tea estates and rubber plantations which were being established by Europeans.

Arabs

People of Arab origin came as traders and began to settle in the coastal towns and villages. They brought Islam with them, and today they work mainly as fishermen and merchants.

The CIIth Indian Royal Pavilion, Potonnaruwa

Europeans

The final group of people to make their home in Sri Lanka were the Europeans, mainly Dutch, English, and Portuguese settlers. Today these people form a distinct community known as Burghers and live mainly in the urban areas.

Ancient Civilisations

The spread of the Sinhalese civilisation across the island depended on a reliable water supply to ensure the success of the farming methods on which it relied. As a result, the rulers of the time organised the building of one of the most sophisticated irrigation systems that the world had seen. Great dams of earth were constructed which fed a network of canals. One of these dams, built in about 470 A.D. was nearly seven kilometres long, up to 18 metres high and covered an area of 18 square kilometres. A great canal, known as the 'Giant's Canal' which was 12 metres wide, carried the water almost 90 kilometres to the ancient capital of Anuradhapura. Some idea of the engineering skill involved in the building of this system can be given by the fact that in parts the gradient of this canal had a fall of only 7.8 centimetres for each kilometre.

Sri Lanka at this time was not ruled entirely by a single king. There were great leaders who controlled large areas of the island. However, their authority was never absolute and a wealthy middle-class of landowners existed. Many of the Buddhist monasteries were able to buy and sell land. The Buddhist religion also acted as a modifying force on the caste system which had been introduced from India. The caste system places some people in such a lowly position in society that they are considered untouchable by others. The Buddhists regarded this attitude as being unjust because they saw all people as being equal.

The Indian past — two Hindu temples face a Colombo street

The greatest threat to Sri Lankan independence came from the Hindu States of southern India in the fifth and sixth centuries A.D. At this time the Tamil settlements in Sri Lanka gave support to Indian invaders. But it was not until 1017 A.D. that the island came under direct Indian rule for the first and only time in its history. Indian rule lasted for only 75 years, but traces of the conflict between Tamil and Sinhalese remain to this day with Tamil separatists fighting for an independent state in the north of the island.

European Rulers

The first Europeans to have an influence in Sri Lanka were the Portuguese. They converted some of the Sri Lankan rulers to Catholicism and although they were interested more in trade than conquest, they occupied a number of coastal areas. These developments saw the shifting of the capital and the consolidation of the Sinhala Kingdom in the hills, with Kandy as the capital.

In an effort to get rid of the Portuguese an alliance was formed with the Dutch who were interested in expanding their spice trade throughout Asia. In 1656 the Dutch captured Colombo and drove out the Portuguese. Under the Dutch rule Sri Lanka became known as Ceylon, and because of their policy of treating each group in the island as separate people with their own laws, it was during this time that the Moorish population rose to greater importance.

The British conquest of Sri Lanka began in 1796 when they removed the Dutch from the island. But it was not until 1815 that a treaty was signed between the native rulers of Sri Lanka and the British colonists. The British introduced the plantation crops of coffee, tea and rubber. They also brought in Tamil plantation

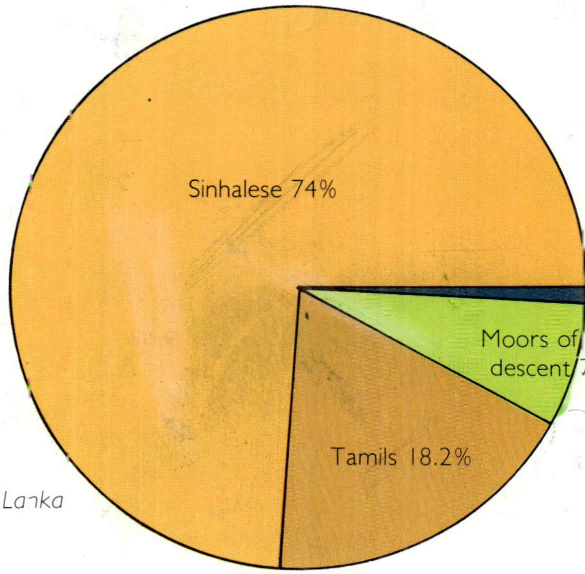

Peoples of Sri Lanka

workers from southern India. These workers were used to build roads, harbours and railways, and later as resident workers on plantations, and so helped to maintain the British grip on the island. Despite a strong nationalist feeling, British rule was regarded generally as a benefit and a series of reforms resulted in Sri Lankans being the first people under direct Colonial rule to be granted universal suffrage, that is one person, one vote.

Independence

Compared with events in India and Burma, the moves towards independence in Sri Lanka were peaceful. Sri Lanka became independent on 4 February 1948 and was declared a republic in 1972.

Constitution and Government

The Government of Sri Lanka was based on the system used in the United Kingdom. Originally there were two houses in the Parliament, but the upper house, or Senate was abolished in 1971.

Members of Parliament are elected by a system of proportional representation for a period of six years under the leadership of the Prime Minister and the President. The President is elected by the people and must receive more than 50 per cent of the votes cast at his election. As well as being the Head of Government, the President is also Head of the Armed Forces, but may not serve for more than two terms, that is, twelve years at any one time.

The island is divided into 24 districts which are run by government appointed agents. Each district has its own council while each of the twelve major cities also have their own separate municipal councils.

Agriculture

The crop for which Sri Lanka was first famous was cinnamon which is a spice made from the inner bark of a type of laurel tree. Soon after the arrival of the British, however, coffee began to be grown in plantations and became an important part of the economy. But in the late nineteenth century a fungus disease of the coffee bush had destroyed many of the plantations which were then turned over to tea growing.

After India, Sri Lanka is the world's largest producer and exporter of tea. Between eighty and ninety per cent of the 220,000 tonnes of tea produced each year is exported and it accounts for the largest part of Sri Lanka's foreign earnings.

Most of the tea is grown in the wet zone and the best teas are grown on the higher slopes, often at heights of over 1,200 metres. The best teas are still picked by hand although harvesting machines are available. The leaves are then withered using either natural or artificial heat for about 20 hours after which they are crushed to remove the bitter juices. Following this the leaves are separated and spread out in special areas where they are dampened and allowed to ferment for about two hours. They are then finally dried, sorted and packed into large wooden chests which are lined with metal foil to keep the tea in perfect condition.

Tea production is almost entirely controlled by the Government, and the tea trade mostly by the private sector. Tea is sold in large auctions in Colombo, and may be in bulk form, packeted, or even as tea bags.

Tea pickers at work on a plantation

Drying coconuts in the sun

Other Crops

The other two main plantation crops are rubber and coconuts. Rubber growing began in 1876 and the first export left Sri Lanka in 1900. The rubber plantations on the island are some of the oldest in the world and today a modern Rubber Research Institute investigates new methods of production.

The largest plantations are those which grow coconuts. The coconut palm is the source of many raw materials. Its leaves can be used for thatch on houses, and ropes are made from the fibres which are removed from the fruit itself. Coconut oil is widely used in cooking, and in soap and detergent making, while the sap of the tree is used to make a drink called toddy, or arrak. Dried coconut kernals, known as dessicated coconut is a major export to all parts of the world.

Other commercial crops, that is those not used for food, are sugarcane, tobacco, cotton, cinnamon, pepper, citronella and nutmeg.

Rice is the main food crop and is grown on the paddy system. In the past animals, especially buffaloes were used to cultivate the fields, but now the main form of power is provided by tractors.

Agricultural concerns employ nearly half of Sri Lanka's workforce.

Rubber trees are cut to release latex

Walls are woven from the fronds of the coconut palm

Older Forms of Farming

Although not widely practised today, *chena* cultivation was at one time the main form of agriculture in the highland regions. Chena is a form of slash-and-burn agriculture which is a common method of food production in parts of Asia. The farmer clears an area of forest by burning it during the dry season. In the clear patch of ground that results, the crop is planted. Crops included watermelon, pumpkin, beans and grains. The crops grow quickly using the ash from the fires as a fertiliser. There are two main disadvantages of this system. The first is that the cleared ground is easily washed away during heavy rains and in parts this erosion has become a serious threat to the future of many forests. The second disadvantage is that the farmer must spend a lot of time protecting the crops from birds which eat the seed and from wild animals such as pigs, deer, and elephants which can devastate the growing plants. Each evening sentries are posted around the crop to drive away the animals with rattles, firecrackers and sometimes guns. There are even special songs sung by the sentries to help them stay awake during the long night. These songs are known as *pel kavi*, or the songs of the huts.

Industry

Manufacturing industry is of growing importance, but the island suffers from a lack of raw materials. Despite this there is a petroleum refinery and a vehicle assembly plant.

Most of the traditional industries are based on the processing of Sri Lanka's agricultural products. The Government is encouraging investment from overseas companies and a number of industrial estates have been built for use by private firms.

The main secondary industry is the production of textiles and clothing which form the next major export after tea. Other goods produced include pottery and ceramics, paper, cement, vegetable oils, chemicals including fertilisers, and leather goods.

The calico market, Colombo

Transport and Communications

Roads

Travel throughout Sri Lanka is reasonably easy using the island's 25,000 kilometres of roads. There are over half a million vehicles of all types from private cars and motorcycles to buses and lorries.

Railways

The railways are government-owned and run on broad-gauge track. Colombo is the main railway centre and serves over 1,400 kilometres of track.

The port area of Colombo

Travel Overseas

The national airline of Sri Lanka is called Air Lanka and operates out of the international airport at Katunayaka Airport near Colombo. Many foreign airlines have regular scheduled flights to the island and this is an important part of the development of Sri Lanka's tourist trade.

Colombo is one of the busiest shipping ports in Asia. The Sri Lankan Shipping Organisation operates its own ships and also acts as brokers and charter agents for sea transport groups around the world. Cruise liners are regular callers at Sri Lankan ports.

Religion and Festivals

Sri Lanka is a land of many customs and rituals which stem from the main religion of the island which is Buddhism. Many of the festivals involve great colourful processions which the Sri Lankans call *Peraheras*. Perhaps the most famous of these is Perahera of the Sacred Tooth held in August each year.

Religions of Sri Lanka

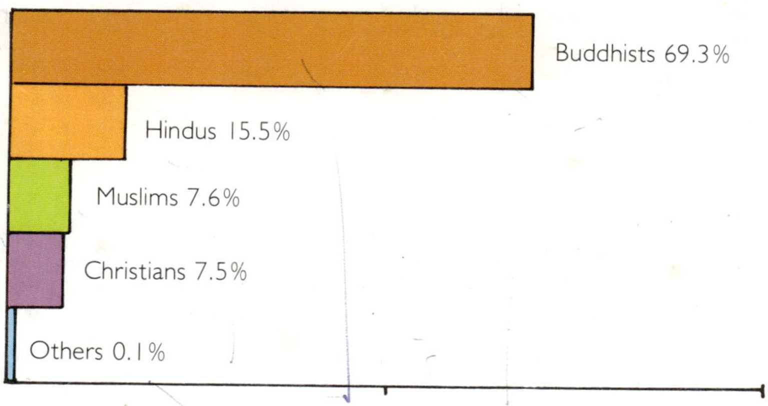

The Perahera of the Sacred Tooth, Kandy

Tradition tells how a tooth of Buddha was brought to Sri Lanka by an Indian Princess called Hemamala who concealed the relic in her hair and disguised herself as a pilgrim. This religious relic was so important that wars were fought for it. The tooth was put into a golden casket and kept in a special temple. Today the tooth is in the town of Kandy. Originally the tooth was taken around the city each year in a procession which lasted up to two weeks. But now only a replica is used because the original is too valuable to risk losing. The replica is carried on the back of an elephant which is decorated all over with colourful cloths and even electric light bulbs. The main procession is followed by groups of devil dancers, school children, acrobats, fire-eaters and other performers. At the end of this festival a sacred sword is used to cut a circle in the river at Kandy. From within this circle four pots are filled and preserved until the following year. It is said that should any of these pots become dry during the year it is a sign of bad luck.

For Buddhists the two most important days of the year are known as Visakha Puja and it is a time when they celebrate both the birth and the death of Buddha. These celebrations take place at the time of the full moon in May. Apart from the usual processions, there are pantomines and even concerts of rock music in the streets. Throughout the island people light special lanterns which often use coconut oil as the fuel. Small roadside stalls are built and furnished with chairs and tables for weary revellers who will also receive free food and drink.

Ornate figures crowd Hindu temples

Hindu Festivals

The festival at Kataragama attracts people of all religions, but it is mainly a Hindu festival. Many Hindus carry out acts of self-mutilation such as suspending themselves by hooks buried in their skin, or thrusting small spears through their cheeks and tongues. Many practice fire-walking without any sign of injury to their bare feet. All this is followed by another procession and a water-cutting ceremony like that at Kandy. Other Hindu celebrations include Deepavali which takes place in October and during which time Hindu houses are re-furnished and new clothes are worn. The festival marks the beginning of the financial year.

Muslim Festivals

There are also many Muslim festivals, but these tend to be quieter and are less public affairs. The birth of the Prophet Mohammad is celebrated in December in the festival of *Milad-um-Nabi*. Ramadan is observed by Muslims in Sri Lanka as it is elsewhere by fasting during the hours of daylight for one month. The festival of Id-ul-Fitr marks the end of Ramadan with a feast and the giving of gifts.

The Pot Dance, Kandy

The Sinhalese New Year

The Sinhalese New Year takes place in April and is celebrated by all Sri Lankans whatever their religion. The date and the time of the New Year are both mathematically determined as is the time of the end of the old year. There may be a gap of a few hours between the end of the old year and the beginning of the new, and this gap is known as the *nona gahte* or neutral period. During this time Sri Lankans take part in acts of religious worship. Before the New Year arrives houses are cleaned and lamps are lit, and at the turn of the year a new fire is lit and new clothes put on. Money may be exchanged and people's heads annointed with a mixture of oil and spices. The New Year is also a time when sports and games are played in many villages.

The Pilgrimage to Adam's Peak

Adam's Peak is said to be a holy mountain by all the major religious groups in Sri Lanka. The Buddhists believe believe that it was visited by Buddha himself and call the peak *Sri Pada*, or 'the sacred footprint'. The Hindus claim that the rock preserves the footprint of Lord Shiva, while Christians believe that the footprint was left by an early Christian missionary to southern India called St Thomas. The Muslims say that the mountain is where Adam first walked on the Earth. Whatever the truth, thousands of pilgrims make the climb of 2,200 metres up a steep rocky path each year to pay their respects at the shrine.

Education

Education is undertaken by central government and organised in 31 regional centres. Of nearly 10,000 schools, only 400 are privately owned.

Children begin their schooling in a kindergarten at about six years of age, but many children in country areas stay at home to work on the fields much of the time, even though education is free to all.

Primary and secondary schools provide tuition in academic subjects such as maths, science, and art. Some students may go to technical colleges to study for trade qualifications such as boatbuilding, or gem cutting, or to study in one of 9 universities. Students are taught in the Sinhalese language, and 86 per cent of the population are able to read and write.

Health and Welfare

Basic medical facilities are free to all Sri Lankans, but people can choose to be treated privately. There are about 500 hospitals with the main hospital being in Colombo, where there are advanced facilities for treating all forms of illness from heart disease to rabies. Medicines are obtained from chemists and drug stores, some of which are government-owned and run.

Herbal medicines are also widely used in Sri Lanka and many people choose to be treated by Ayurvedic doctors at the Government Ayurvedic Hospital. Homeopatnic treatment is available at one government hospital.

Many people drink bottled water, or the juice of the king coconut which is known as *thambili*.

Beaten brass work

Arts and Crafts

Sri Lankan craftsmen have always produced fine work for both decorative and practical purposes in a variety of materials. Wood carving is one of the most ancient crafts and pieces of furniture often have designs taken from traditional stories carved into their various panels. Wood carvings may be plain or coloured with dyes and paints. Some of the most colourful pieces are the masks of the devil dancers. In the past, carvings in ivory and tortoise-shell were also popular, but now that animals are officially protected in many parts of the world the making of these products is discouraged.

Precious metals such as gold and silver are used to make intricate pieces of jewellery, while brass is often used for casting small sculptures, vases, trays, other table ware and decorative items.

Pottery has become, in recent years, an item as much for the tourist as for the house-holder. The individual craftsmen still produce their wares in the traditional way on wheels turned by hand and fired in kilns built of brick. However there are now a number of government funded factories where these items are mass produced, although much of the decoration is still applied by hand.

The same is true for much of the textile trade, where batik cloths are now mainly produced in factories even though much of the work is still done by hand. Lacemaking, introduced by the Portuguese, is another traditional, manual skill which is dying out, although there are various places, such as Galle, where the genuine hand-made article can still be bought.

Basket and mat making are among the few traditional crafts which have yet to be mechanised. Much of the produce of these cottage industries is sold at the many fairs which take place each year around the country.

Preparing to load ceramics for a trip to the market

Fresh food is plentiful; markets are always busy

Food

Sri Lanka has absorbed many dishes into its traditions from other parts of the world. Chief among these are the pastries, biscuits and breads from Europe and particularly from the lands of its old colonial rulers, the Dutch and the Portuguese. The Moors, too, have influenced the native methods of cooking things such as rice.

The greatest influences, however, have come from India. Rice is the staple food for most and can be cooked in a variety of ways as either a savoury or a sweet dish. As in India, curries are popular. They can be mild or hot depending on the blend of spices used. Curries can be based on meat, eggs, vegetables, or fish and each locality has its own special dish. Coconut oil and milk is widely used in the preparation of many dishes and the grated flesh of the coconut is often used as a garnish.

There are always plenty of fresh vegetables for sale in the markets and these are often served finely grated as a side dish. Fresh fruit is a popular dessert. There are also sweet puddings which are usually based on rice, flour, milk and various spices.

Kerosene for sale!

Sport and Recreation

The most popular sports in Sri Lanka are cricket and rugby. The cricket season runs from September to April. Rugby is played for the rest of the year. Both sports draw large and enthusiastic crowds. Football is also played throughout the island, but there is no national team to enter world competitions. Badminton, squash and tennis are also very popular and a number of competitors in these sports have international status. Rowing and golf are also followed. Many of the sporting events and the teams are sponsored by commerical firms which operate in the islands.

Hunting for sport is not allowed anywhere in Sri Lanka, but there is fine fishing in the rivers and lakes as well as offshore where game fishing is mainly a tourist activity.

There are many art galleries which have traditional works on display as well as many by modern Sri Lankan artists such as George Keyt and Senaka Senanayake. Most major centres have well maintained museums which display the history of Sri Lanka.

Sri Lanka has several daily and weekly newspapers of which most appear in Sinhala, but English and Tamil are also represented.

There are two television channels which broadcast news entertainment and children's programmes. The Sri Lanka Broadcasting Corporation also operates a number of local and overseas radio services. Over 400 theatres and cinemas put on both traditional and modern performances.

The formal botanical gardens, Colombo

Gazetteer

Official name: Sri Lanka (Sri Lanka Janarajaya)

Constitution: Democratic Socialist Republic

Head of State: The Executive President (J. R. Jayawardene)

Head of Government: The President

Official language: Sinhala. English is also a national language and Tamil is used in the north and east.

Capital City: Colombo

Area: 65,610 sq. km.

Population: 14.9 million (1981)

Highest mountain: Pidurutalagala, 2,524 metres

Longest river: Mahaweli, 333 km.

Climate: Equatorial, i.e. no clearly defined seasons, but is subject to the monsoon.
Annual average temperatures and rainfall for Colombo: Jan. 26°C, July 27°C. Rainfall - 2,400 mm.

Weights and Measures: The metric system is used

Currency: The unit is the Sri Lankan *rupee*. 1 *rupee* = 100 cents

Religion: Buddhism is the main religion

Airports and Shipping: Air Lanka is the Sri Lankan international airline. The main airport is Colombo International at the town of Katunayake.
There are ferry services from southern India to Talaimannar. Colombo is the main port.

Agricultural production: Main crops are tea, rubber, coconuts, rice

Main exports: Tea, textiles, rubber, coconut and coconut products

Main imports: Petroleum, industrial machinery, motor vehicles

Main trading partners: Japan, Saudi Arabia, Iran, UK

Treaties and Alliances: Sri Lanka is a member of:
The Commonwealth
The United Nations
The Non-Aligned Movement
The Colombo Plan

The flag of Sri Lanka: A yellow background has three panels. The largest (maroon) has a gold lion holding a sword and in each corner is a gold leaf.

Index